THE EQUESTRIAN JOURNAL
For the Thinking Rider

Monthly, Weekly, and Daily Guided Pages Designed to Help You:

Record Your Training Experiences
Practice Visualizations
Develop Awareness
Track Habits
Plan Your Goals
Create Action Steps
Improve Memory and Retention
Unlock Knowledge from Observations
Gain Perspective on Progress
Focus on What's Next
Fulfill Your Potential

created by Catherine Respess

THIS JOURNAL IS DEDICATED TO EQUESTRIANS WHO STRIVE TO GET MORE FROM EACH EXPERIENCE WITH THEIR HORSE.

I spent years in the barn scribbling notes in my calendar, personal diaries, and even a couple of blogs. The habit caught on from my high school work-study program that required a semester of observations about a horse I trained for course credit. I still have that journal and it's great to look back on how much I've learned!

Over the years, my journals evolved from those disorganized scribbles, my observations began to improve, and a whole new world of equine knowledge emerged for me. Even though my entries frequently help me track progress and make decisions about my horse, I thought there had to be a journal that could help me organize and unlock knowledge from my observations.

After researching and experimenting with many styles of journals, I couldn't find a perfect solution. I created The Equestrian Journal as a way to process our experiences, develop our awareness, strengthen our partnerships, and fulfill our potential with horses.

I'm very proud of how The Equestrian Journal has developed over the years! We offer Accelerator Journal Coaching, 3 types of journal bindings, a digital journal to use on your tablet or phone, many alternative page options, and custom designed journals. Please let me know if you have any specific requests or would enjoy a custom option for your program. I love hearing from my "journalers."

Be sure to check out our Certified Partner Program - it's a sprinkle of sponsorship, a dash of affiliate alliance, and a big scoop of added value to the services offered by educators, clinicians, bodyworkers, coaches, and trainers.
https://www.theequestrianjournal.com/partnerships

Please feel welcome to post your successes on Instagram, Amazon, or our Facebook page:
www.facebook.com/theequestrianjournal.

You may enjoy using some of these hashtags:
#TheEquestrianJournal #journalthat #observeyourhorse #Awareness #takenotes #horses #horsecare #horsetraining #notes #journaling #horselover #makingadifference #ponies #horse #equestrian #equestrianworld #horseback #horseaddict #horsebackriding #horselife #journal #horsejournal #horsejourney #stories #experience #habittracker #rateyourride #trainyourmind #shiftyourattention #journaltodiscover #betterthanbefore #mindfulness #confidentrider #tagyourtrainer #followforinspiration #journalingjourney
#everybitcounts #gratitude

For the Horse,

Catherine Respess

"Your horse's body is an open book....

if you take the time to learn to read it.

Knowledge is a powerful contributor to

wellness in horses.

There is no better teacher than the horse

and no better student than the

rider who wishes the best for his horse

and uses all his senses to understand

and care for him better."

- Manolo Mendez
www.ManoloMendez.com

TABLE OF CONTENTS

WHY JOURNAL?

You are a dedicated horse owner, but when you reflect back on your horse's history, the days blend together. Your recollection of training sessions or details about your horse's experiences are not what they could be.

We know from studies on the process of recall that each time the mind constructs a past event, the brain networks change in ways that actually alter the memory. Training professionals have long dealt with the challenge of improving their students' retention after the training experiences. This studied by German psychologist Hermann Ebbinghaus in 1885. His discovery was that 70% information is forgotten within 24-48 hours.

Have you had an experience with your horse that enlightened you? Did you reach a training milestone? You are sure that you want to learn from your past, but sometimes we lose track of that knowledge simply because of the way our brain recalls our memories when we do not record what we have learned.

JOURNALING IS A MEANS FOR RECORDING PERSONAL THOUGHTS, DAILY EXPERIENCES, AND EVOLVING INSIGHTS.

According to the American Psychological Association, a regular habit of writing helps reduce intrusive mental block and improve working memory, allowing you to use all of your brainpower to better comprehend critical elements of information. Add the advantage of reading earlier reflections and subtle themes can develop into powerful insights.

In addition to all of these wonderful benefits, keeping a journal specifically about your horse allows you to track habits you wish to cultivate, behavior patterns, techniques that work, and your improvement over time.

SHARE YOUR JOURNAL WITH YOUR TEAM.
Your instructor and your horse's farrier, veterinarian, and body workers can all learn something from insights on what is working or not working. Your insights may even lead to a better connection as a team and a better education for you.

PRACTICE VISUALIZATIONS - TRIPLE EFFECT
Devote a little time before and after a lesson or session with your horse to experience a tripling effect.
1st PRACTICE WITH YOUR HORSE on your own or in a lesson with your trainer.
2nd RECORD YOUR EXPERIENCE for a second chance to let the lesson sink in or even capture insight
  that you may have missed in the moment.
3rd REVISIT YOUR NOTES before your next ride and bring yourself back to the wisdom and feel
  gained during the previous session.
You'll feel more prepared and focused when you turn one lesson into three!

EXPERIENCE THESE BENEFITS:

CONNECT THE PUZZLE PIECES

Observing and tracking the fine details means considering each discovery as if it were a piece of the puzzle. The factors that influence your behavior and your horse's behavior mean something. Note the strategies that work and make time for the components of the program that help us progress.

Construct a meaningful picture from the pieces you gather. As a result, you'll have a better sense of where to start each day and how to make progress.

CLARIFY YOUR THOUGHTS AND FEELINGS.

Do you ever seem all jumbled up inside and unsure of what you want or feel? Taking a few minutes to jot down the unedited version your thoughts will quickly get you in touch with your internal world. Free yourself from the emotional charge and physical blocks in order to dance with your horse in this way of pure communication.

KNOW YOURSELF AND YOUR HORSE BETTER.

Routinely writing about your experiences at the barn or when traveling with your horse, improves your awareness, understanding, and partnership with your horse. The record of these events will clarify what makes you both feel happy and confident.

REDUCE STRESS AND ANXIETY.

Writing about setbacks or intense emotions helps to release the resulting feelings. By doing so you will feel calmer and better able to stay in the present. You may even change your perspective and improve your outlook with the realization that the setback wasn't as significant as it felt in the moment. When current circumstances appear insurmountable, look back on dilemmas that you resolved and learn from your experience.

SUPPORT THE MENTAL WORK OF LEARNING

Research by Pam Mueller and Daniel Oppenheimer demonstrates that students who organize and summarize new knowledge on paper by writing their notes, actually learn more. Most people can type faster than they write, and as a result they transcribe what they hear as opposed capturing the information as succintly as possible using the learning process called assimilation. The practice of drawing or diagraming has also been proven to be a very effective memory rentention technique for the same reason.

SOLVE PROBLEMS MORE EFFECTIVELY.

Typically we problem solve from a left-brained, analytical perspective. But sometimes the answer can only be found by engaging right-brained creativity and intuition. Writing unlocks these other capabilities and affords the opportunity for unexpected solutions to seemingly unsolvable problems.

Experiment with a "story-telling" style of journaling to bring you back into the moment that you are recalling. By considering the details that help you remember what you felt, saw, and heard, you may stumble upon a valuable solution!

THE EQUESTRIAN JOURNAL GUIDE:

Find the routine that works for you and I promise you that your horse will thank you for paying attention. Even in a rush, you can write a few lines of information that will help you in the future. The Equestrian Journal includes three methods for organizing your thoughts and details about your horse: Monthly, Weekly, and Daily.

PLAN YOUR GOALS
Address goals big and small. If you have a grand ideas for your future - fantastic! However, keep in mind that progress occurs incrementally in the form of micro goals. Challenge yourself to write down those VERY small steps.

MONTHLY
Four months are provided in case you commence your journal mid month. The MONTH IN LINE column is for those who enjoy an additional organizational option.

ORGANIZE THE VARIOUS COMPONENTS OF YOUR TRAINING PROGRAM
We all juggle a lot of factors in our horses daily lives. Keep track of what needs to be completed and what is or isn't working. Plan ahead for a fun outing or a competition. Keep your horse interested in progress by coordinating a variety of experiences.

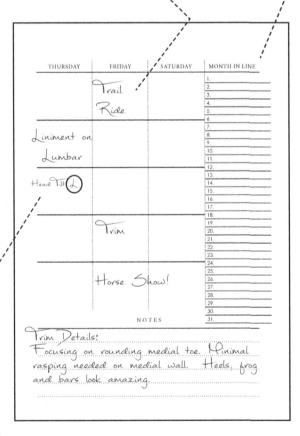

NOTE OBSERVATIONS
Convey accurate details to a practitioner. Record your horse's preferences. Unlock knowledge in your observations.

RECORD APPOINTMENTS
All in one place history of body work, veterinary, or farrier appointments.

WEEKLY

GAIN PERSPECTIVE ON PROGRESS TO FULFILL YOUR POTENTIAL

Start each week by setting your intention. You may wish to look back on the previous week for inspiration. Many riders feel stagnated in their routine or lose momentum because they fail to recall where they left off the previous week or before a break.

Return to reflect on the goals you've set for yourself. You will be amazed at what you have overcome. This is a positive motivator for your continued success. Keep writing, and review entries to see how you and your horse have developed.

DEVELOP AWARENESS & STRENGTHEN YOUR PARTNERSHIP

Look back at previous entries for details that may be connected. You'll start to notice patterns and connections, gaining valuable insight to gain a better understanding of your equine partner.

HABIT TRACKING

Every day, we practice good and bad habits, sometimes without thinking. Each repetition enforces a behavior and strengthens the pathways in your brain related to it.

Add quality to your life by setting a goal and creating action steps to reach that goal. Be firm about your choices right now. Avoid reverting to habits, patterns, and influences that weren't helping you evolve.

Use this page to remind yourself why you even decided to make a change. Stay positive about what is to come by being consistent with your change now. Revisit this page throughout the week to keep up with your progress.

TRAINER NOTES

Share your journal with your trainer or coach for another perspective on what is working and is not working. This insight could clarify communication with your trainer and contribute to your education in a powerful manner.

WEEK ONE

What are your goals this week?

Drink more water

Work on my shoulders – L- Shoulder more down and
back. R-Shoulder more open and forward

On a scale of 1 - 10, how was your horse this week and why?

8 – Catawba is offering the canter constantly! I feel
like he's proud of his own progress and better under-
stands our goals.

What did you learn about your horse or yourself from observations?

Getting my shoulders in better postion actually helps
Catawba to recycle the energy in the canter!

HABIT/ ACTION STEPS	S	M	T	W	TH	F	S
Yoga	x				x		x
Visualize Shoulder Position		x			x		
Groom on Balance Pad			x			x	
Water - Bring a Bottle			x		x	x	

What do you want to focus on next week?

Ride a first level test!

Trainer Notes:

Huge progress in the canter work! Keep working on small circles and experiment
with different half halts in the canter. Good work!

DAILY PAGES

Summarizing information is another way of reviewing and critically thinking about what you have learned. After each session, record your observations and new knowledge within 24-hours to maximize the precision of your recollection.

Since most horses have a day of rest, I have only included 6 daily pages for each of the 13-weeks in this journal. Please utilize the extra pages in the back of the journal if you need more space.

NOTE YOUR OBSERVATIONS HORSE & RIDER
- Energy level before/after training?
- Level of stress?
- Level of confidence?
- Level of motivation?
- Muscle soreness?
- Nutrition pre/post workout?

EQUIPMENT
- What did you use?
- What changed?
- What needs to change?

BASED ON SUBTLE BEHAVIORAL INDICATORS,
is your horse happy, tense, tired, guarded, or responsive?

- What is his attitude?
- Any discomfort?
- What are his preferences? Responses?
- Eating Habits?
- Turnout Schedule?

DIAGRAM
The observation diagram is available for you to note changes in your horse's body or details that you wish to remember.

The diagram is intended to be faint enough to write over top if you need more space for your observations on a particular day.

NEXT STEPS
Give yourself an objective in the next lesson based on the progress made today.

Keep the routine fresh and interesting while setting yourself up for a great next session.

Daily | Tuesday, April 1, 2019

Observations

Catawba had a little rub on his left haunch... it looks like he might have been scratching himself on a tree. I did a masterson session while I was grooming him and got some big releases on that haunch and on the right front under neck.

I'm really pleased that despite all the rain, we are not seeing any thrush at all.

Very thankful that Mike is picking foot when he brings the horses inside after turnout.

Points of the Session & Diagram Space

Set up a new pole exercise on a serpentine and included a change of direction to a 10 meter circles to shoulder in halfway down the long side.

The change of direction from the larger circle which was a nice way to balance him for the 5-in 5-in out of the 10 meter circle sets him up really well and then I proceeded down the longside straight.

I also found this worked well to do another change of direction from B to E and ride haunches in down to the 10 meter circle.

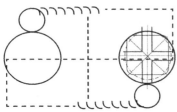

Catawba seemed to enjoy the addition of the poles - he loves to jump!

I did warm up out on the trail at the walk/ trot/ canter and then brought him to the arena. I introduced the exercise at the walk and then played with it at the trot and canter :)

What do you want to focus on next session?

I'll be sure to lift these poles up next week so that he can hop over something more.

POINTS OF THE SESSION

How did you feel? How did your horse feel? What did your horse convey?

Visualize the exercises or sensations that were successful. If you captured a pearl of wisdom, record the phrasing that resonated with you or draw a diagram to preserve the feeling. Remember visualizations are often as effective as the actual practice!

WHAT DIDN'T WORK?

Do not beat yourself up or make judgments. Write down your observations and move on. This unflinching record will be a big help later when evaluating the big picture.

TRAINING

- Comments on how training went
- Time of training?
- Session length?
- Indoor, outdoor, trail, clinic, or competition?
- Exercises performed?
- Rate of effort during training?
- Quality rating?
- Variety?
- Highlights of training session?

RECOMMENDED ABBREVIATIONS

S-der	shoulder
H-d	hind
S-in	shoulder in
H-in	haunches in
R	right
L	left
L-y	leg yield

NEED HELP GETTING STARTED?

Schedule an Accelerator Journal Coaching session to review your ride and receive a "leg-up" on the process of journaling. Visit the website or Call/ Text/ Email Catherine to set up your session!

www.TheEquestrianJournal.com | 404.457.4629 | Catherine@RedMareEnterprises.com

DESCRIPTIVE EMOTIONS

The words below are provided to offer you inspiration as you consider what you wish to say.

Caring	Amused	Animated	Tense	Threatened	Sore	Curious
Helpful	Cheerful	Annoyed	Nervous	Anxious	Powerless	Clever
Secure	Comical	Agitated	Intimidated	Helpless	Shaky	Inquisitive
Attentive	Silly	Frustrated	Fearful	Miserable	Sick	Motivated
Considerate	Happy	Mad	Panicked	Heartbroken	Frail	Stimulated
Friendly	Optimistic	Critical	Shaky	Depressed	Exhausted	Active
Kind	Alive	Resentful	Horrified	Terrible	Fragile	Energetic
Understanding	Delighted	Disgusted	Terrified	Crushed	Vulnerable	Intrigued
Giving	Spontaneous	Outraged	Flumoxed	Low	Defenseless	Engaged
Supportive	Imaginative	Furious	Mixed up	Gloomy	Discouraged	Constructive
Connected	Whimsical	Livid	Unsure	Disturbed	Overwhelmed	Productive
Tender	Joyful	Bitter	Uncomfortable	Distressed	Trapped	Creative
Loving	Energized	Timid	Troubled	Crushed	Desperate	Eager
Joined	Cheerful	Uneasy	Perplexed	Hurt		Bold
Attached	Exicted	Insecure	Disoriented	Unhappy	Inspired	Artistic
Spirited	Bouncy	Cowardly	Stunned	Thirsty	Inventive	Fascinated
Playful	Lively	Worried	Shocked	Hungry	Ambitious	Confident
Relaxed	Elated	Afriad	Stuck	Tired	Absorbed	Focused
Glad	Estatic	Worn out	Lost	Run-Down	Obsessed	Determined
Light-hearted						

"By recording your dreams and goals on paper, you set in motion the process of becoming the person you most want to be. Put your future in good hands—your own."

- Mark Victor Hansen

PLANNING YOUR GOALS

What do you want?
Sometimes it is hard to answer this question, but with a little probing, you can uncover your goals and motivations.

Continue to grow as a rider, develop my horse to her potential

What's holding you back?
The wonderful thing about journaling is we can analize our thought patterns and discover the actions that hold us back from our goals.

My own stiffness, ↓ strength, time lack of regular training

What is it costing you to continue holding back?
Are your actions, thoughts, and habits impeding your progress?

How could you show up differently?
How can you change your behavior to become the person who can accomplish your goals?

More regular investment in fitness / lessons

What is a new perspective that you could adopt right now?
Looking at your goals from an outside perspective can give you direction on more positive changes.

Not sure

What is the most meaningful action you could take right now?
Plan out your next best action that take you to your goals.

Regular stretching / exercise

What new habits will you put in place right now?
Think of habits as small successes that can change your reality

Stretch at least 2x/wk + start yoga

What new skills or support systems will ensure your success?
Consider your resources and if you need a new system of support.

DRT / Books

MONTH: March

SUNDAY	MONDAY	TUESDAY	WEDNESDAY
	1 work on compress Laurie canter→walk Ride clean △ R→ kick L-R	**2** learn Ride- snaffle - trans in gait- - Med to coll trot coll canter- walk	**3** Jill ※
7 - Double - mediums canter/walk coll trot felt ok, need ↑ jump ☆	**8** snaffle - work off seat ↑↓ trot - coll canter/ walk, coll trot Hack	**9** EVA ride ♡	**10** Laurie Ride △ R-L stretness ↑ coll ♡ half pass Double ※
14 snaffle trans-halt coll canter→walk outside good energy ☆	**15** Double Short ride ↑ energy medium trot work-good! ☆	**16** Laurie Ride GREAT - Double clean △ R-L a few L-R/lots of bucks (really good)	**17** OFF
21 Jill Ride	**22** Double - half pass ↑supple - control shldr hanches in center collect - on circle+ Strt line, wheelbarrow vs. dolly	**23** shldr/hanches in - work on coll/ext canter, ↑energy in coll canter walk pir.	**24** First changes! yay!
28 Jill ride	**29** snaffle - Franklin balls - I'm stiff in hips + helps deepen my seat	**30** OFF	**31** Jill

NOTES

※ Needs to push behind
☆ super collect canter
3/23 - a little tired! work on ↑ ease of coll energy in
coll canter, compress energy so change/medium is a release -
seat teacup vs. bowl

THURSDAY	FRIDAY	SATURDAY	MONTH IN LINE
4 Jill ✶	5 OFF ✶	6 Ride NO stirrups double - trot-halt - half pass - shlr in - coll center	1. coughing
			2. good energy, a bit tense, less coughing
			3.
			4.
			5.
			6. Nice coll canters to Ⓛ
11 Ella ride -saddle fit -farrier	12 OFF	13 Snaffle WOW Ride ↑ medium trot + canter - SO GOOD	7. Needs ↑ jump/imp. ok
			8. ✶ Nice coll canter
			9.
			10.
			11.
			12.
18 Snaffle stretchy short ride - field good	19 OFF	20 walk- hack :)	13. GREAT RIDE ↑ energy!
			14. good energy
			15. good energy
			16.
			17.
			18.
25 Lianter day medium to coll canters trot, walk ½ pass	24 OFF :) hard walk	27 Snaffle stretchy trot/canter + hack in ~20 field min good	19.
			20.
			21.
			22.
			23.
			24.
Jill	Double	Double - hips stiff - work on move off seat	25.
			26.
			27. Stiff to Ⓛ bend
			28.
			29.
			30.
			31.

NOTES

3/22 great! Focus on shldr/posture, short reins + bring hands frwrd to her, ride from seat, ↑ control of shldr + haunches in canter, half pass → ↑ suppleness + bend whole body around inside leg.

MONTH: April

SUNDAY	MONDAY	TUESDAY	WEDNESDAY
Jill 4	Snaffle 5 short, work on halt, collect, lengthen off seat + thach	OFF 6	Jill 7
Jill			

NOTES

THURSDAY	FRIDAY	SATURDAY	MONTH IN LINE
Jill 8	Dable 9 - work off intuition -great trot/half/canter -harder for lateral	Hack 10 out 11	1.
			2.
			3.
			4.
			5.
			6.
			7.
			8.
			9.
			10.
			11.
			12.
			13.
			14.
			15.
			16.
			17.
			18.
			19.
			20.
			21.
			22.
			23.
			24.
			25.
			26.
			27.
			28.
			29.
			30.
			31.

NOTES

MONTH:

SUNDAY	MONDAY	TUESDAY	WEDNESDAY

NOTES

THURSDAY	FRIDAY	SATURDAY	MONTH IN LINE
			1.
			2.
			3.
			4.
			5.
			6.
			7.
			8.
			9.
			10.
			11.
			12.
			13.
			14.
			15.
			16.
			17.
			18.
			19.
			20.
			21.
			22.
			23.
			24.
			25.
			26.
			27.
			28.
			29.
			30.
			31.

NOTES

MONTH:

SUNDAY	MONDAY	TUESDAY	WEDNESDAY

NOTES

....
....
....
....
....

THURSDAY	FRIDAY	SATURDAY	MONTH IN LINE
			1.
			2.
			3.
			4.
			5.
			6.
			7.
			8.
			9.
			10.
			11.
			12.
			13.
			14.
			15.
			16.
			17.
			18.
			19.
			20.
			21.
			22.
			23.
			24.
			25.
			26.
			27.
			28.
			29.
			30.
			31.

NOTES

"Horsemanship is the art of mastering our own movements, thoughts, emotions and behavior. Not the horse's."

- Mark Rashid

WEEK ONE

What were your goals this week?

Lawrie Training Ride
1 more Double Ride, prep for changes

On a scale of 1 - 10, how was your horse this week and why?

What did you observe about your horse or yourself?

HABIT/ ACTION STEPS	S	M	T	W	TH	F	S

What do you want to focus on next week?

Trainer Notes:

WEEK TWO

What were your goals this week?

....

....

On a scale of 1 - 10, how was your horse this week and why?

....

....

What did you observe about your horse or yourself?

....

....

HABIT/ ACTION STEPS	S	M	T	W	TH	F	S
....							
....							
....							
....							

What do you want to focus on next week?

....

....

Trainer Notes:

....

....

WEEK THREE

What were your goals this week?

....

....

On a scale of 1 - 10, how was your horse this week and why?

....

....

What did you observe about your horse or yourself?

....

....

HABIT/ ACTION STEPS	S	M	T	W	TH	F	S
....							
....							
....							
....							

What do you want to focus on next week?

....

....

Trainer Notes:

....

....

WEEK FOUR

What were your goals this week?

_____

....

....

On a scale of 1 - 10, how was your horse this week and why?

_____

....

....

What did you observe about your horse or yourself?

_____

....

....

HABIT/ ACTION STEPS	S	M	T	W	TH	F	S
....							
....							
....							
....							

What do you want to focus on next week?

_____

....

....

Trainer Notes:

_____

....

....

WEEK FIVE

What were your goals this week?

....

....

On a scale of 1 - 10, how was your horse this week and why?

....

....

What did you observe about your horse or yourself?

....

....

HABIT/ ACTION STEPS	S	M	T	W	TH	F	S
....							
....							
....							
....							

What do you want to focus on next week?

....

....

Trainer Notes:

....

....

WEEK SIX

What were your goals this week?

....

....

On a scale of 1 - 10, how was your horse this week and why?

....

....

What did you observe about your horse or yourself?

....

....

HABIT/ ACTION STEPS	S	M	T	W	TH	F	S
....							
....							
....							
....							

What do you want to focus on next week?

....

....

Trainer Notes:

....

....

WEEK SEVEN

What were your goals this week?

On a scale of 1 - 10, how was your horse this week and why?

What did you observe about your horse or yourself?

HABIT/ ACTION STEPS	S	M	T	W	TH	F	S

What do you want to focus on next week?

Trainer Notes:

WEEK EIGHT

What were your goals this week?

....

....

On a scale of 1 - 10, how was your horse this week and why?

....

....

What did you observe about your horse or yourself?

....

....

HABIT/ ACTION STEPS	S	M	T	W	TH	F	S
....							
....							
....							
....							

What do you want to focus on next week?

....

....

Trainer Notes:

....

....

WEEK NINE

What were your goals this week?

On a scale of 1 - 10, how was your horse this week and why?

What did you observe about your horse or yourself?

HABIT/ ACTION STEPS	S	M	T	W	TH	F	S

What do you want to focus on next week?

Trainer Notes:

WEEK TEN

What were your goals this week?

....

....

....

On a scale of 1 - 10, how was your horse this week and why?

....

....

....

What did you observe about your horse or yourself?

....

....

....

HABIT/ ACTION STEPS	S	M	T	W	TH	F	S
....							
....							
....							
....							

What do you want to focus on next week?

....

....

....

Trainer Notes:

....

....

....

WEEK ELEVEN

What were your goals this week?

....

....

On a scale of 1 - 10, how was your horse this week and why?

....

....

What did you observe about your horse or yourself?

....

....

HABIT/ ACTION STEPS	S	M	T	W	TH	F	S
....							
....							
....							
....							

What do you want to focus on next week?

....

....

Trainer Notes:

....

....

WEEK TWELVE

What were your goals this week?

....

....

On a scale of 1 - 10, how was your horse this week and why?

....

....

What did you observe about your horse or yourself?

....

....

HABIT/ ACTION STEPS	S	M	T	W	TH	F	S
....							
....							
....							
....							

What do you want to focus on next week?

....

....

Trainer Notes:

....

....

WEEK THIRTEEN

What were your goals this week?

....

....

On a scale of 1 - 10, how was your horse this week and why?

....

....

What did you observe about your horse or yourself?

....

....

HABIT/ ACTION STEPS	S	M	T	W	TH	F	S
....							
....							
....							
....							

What do you want to focus on next week?

....

....

Trainer Notes:

....

....

"Choose to be optimistic,

it feels better."

- Dalai Lama

Daily | S M T W TH F S ____ / ____ / 20____

Observations

....

....

Points of the Session & Diagram Space

....

....

What do you want to focus on next session?

....

....

Daily | S M T W TH F S ____ / ____ / 20____

Observations

....

....

Points of the Session & Diagram Space

....

....

What do you want to focus on next session?

....

....

Daily | S M T W TH F S ___ / ___ / 20___

Observations

....

....

Points of the Session & Diagram Space

....

....

What do you want to focus on next session?

....

....

Daily | S M T W TH F S ____ /____ / 20____

Observations

....

....

Points of the Session & Diagram Space

....

....

What do you want to focus on next session?

....

....

"I encourage everyone to explore how little it would take to get the horse to do what is wanted and to get him 100% OK on the inside, before asking anything else of him. These are the laws of horsemanship. These are the laws to live by.

We will not be seeing rollkur after we die, but I do think that horsemanship, the horse-human relationship, is eternal. Just do what you know is good for the horse, and continue to discover how to take a horse that is unsound mentally or physically and by riding him and treating him in the right way, make him sound of mind and body."

- Dr. Deb Bennett
Equine Studies Institute

Daily | S M T W TH F S ____ / ____ / 20____

Observations

....

....

Points of the Session & Diagram Space

....

....

What do you want to focus on next session?

....

....

Daily | S M T W TH F S ____ / ____ / 20____

Observations

....

....

Points of the Session & Diagram Space

....

....

What do you want to focus on next session?

....

....

Daily | S M T W TH F S ____ / ____ / 20____

Observations

....

....

Points of the Session & Diagram Space

....

....

What do you want to focus on next session?

....

....

Daily | S M T W TH F S ____ / ____ / 20____

Observations

_____

....

....

Points of the Session & Diagram Space

_____

....

....

What do you want to focus on next session?

_____

....

....

"We are what we repeatedly do.

Excellence, then, is not an act,

but a habit."

- Aristotle

Daily | S M T W TH F S   3 / 22 / 20

Observations

Work on control of shldrs / hanches in
cantr ᴇ shldr in / hanches in on a circle

Points of the Session & Diagram Space

↑ Suppleness + bend for 1/2 pass
    Wheelbarrel vs. Dolly for control hanches

My shldrs down + back + chest out, uphill
frame held in this posture

↓ Shorter snaffle reins + bring hands forward

What do you want to focus on next session?

Daily | S M T W TH F S 3 / 23 / 20 21

Observations

Work on call canter + ease of call/ext
within canter/trot Tapping à bucks! Trying to
get haunches to come under.

Points of the Session & Diagram Space

Half pass work - move shlds in/haunches in.
Diagonal to half pass)

haunches in +
Point to wall or haunch in + yield to
C-line, ↑ bend around
inside leg

a little sore
- bute + liniment

What do you want to focus on next session?

Need shorter steps + more rich back for
walk pirouette

Daily | S M T W TH F S 3 / 29 / 20 21

Observations

Practiced coll canter + canter walk on diagonal - Sunni
offered a change from L-R (≈ a buck) when coll on a ⊙.
Clean change first try R-L! Worked on trot/halt/back ≈
↑ energy!

Points of the Session & Diagram Space

Body steps to change.
<u>Outside - holds balance/supports + Inside legs thrust/push</u>
Position As you collect for change, collect an outside
hip to send balance to leading leg + prep for change of
balance ↑ energy up to trans, then release outside hip +
bring to girth while cueing change ≈ new outside
leg + half halt on new outside reign. Cue is on
upswing.

- Felt good, liniment
    - shots + banamine after ride

What do you want to focus on next session?

More coord. ≈ aids + more clear

Observations

A little less pep today, tired!. Still good + willing.

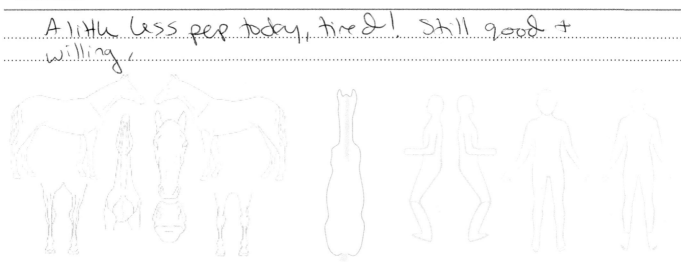

Points of the Session & Diagram Space

- Walk pirouettes - need ↑ energy, weight inside seat + less outside leg not too far back.

- Med / coll canter - uphill is collect downhill to ext, ↑ energy in collect + then release

- Some in medium trot

- ended with great, steady, uphill med trot

- kept losing Ⓛ stirrup in medi trot!

  half pass + med trot

What do you want to focus on next session?

"Accept what the horse offers. It is his interpretation of what we are asking."

- Mark Russell

Observations

My seat felt stiff so I used the Franklin balls to deepen + loosen. Canter depart to (L) from trot stiff + a bit, lots of trans.

Points of the Session & Diagram Space

Worked on sensitivity to my seat + using seat for all aids - worked very well! I need to remember this.

What do you want to focus on next session?

Double + work on coll. again

Daily | S M T W TH F S ____ / ____ / 20____

Observations

_____

. . . .

. . . .

Points of the Session & Diagram Space

_____

. . . .

. . . .

What do you want to focus on next session?

_____

. . . .

. . . .

Daily | S M T W TH F S ____ /____ / 20____

Observations

....

....

Points of the Session & Diagram Space

....

....

What do you want to focus on next session?

....

....

Daily | S M T W TH F S ____ / ____ / 20____

Observations

....

....

Points of the Session & Diagram Space

....

....

What do you want to focus on next session?

....

....

"Elastic musculature is a more sophisticated sign of relaxation than a mere absences of tension. Only horses that are elastic and supple can move with engagement in the haunches and lightness in the forehand."

- Charles De Kunffy

Daily | S M T W TH F S ___ / ___ / 20___

Observations

_____

....

....

Points of the Session & Diagram Space

_____

....

....

What do you want to focus on next session?

_____

....

....

Daily | S M T W TH F S ___ /___ / 20___

Observations

....

....

Points of the Session & Diagram Space

....

....

What do you want to focus on next session?

....

....

Daily | S M T W TH F S ____ / ____ / 20____

Observations

....

....

Points of the Session & Diagram Space

....

....

What do you want to focus on next session?

....

....

Daily | S M T W TH F S ____ / ____ / 20____

Observations

....

....

Points of the Session & Diagram Space

....

....

What do you want to focus on next session?

....

....

"Our preoccupation with the horse's resistances misses the real point on so many levels. Blaming the horse for resistance is shooting the messenger. What then is resistance? Resistance is when the contents and the aspirations of your mind do not agree with reality.

Every resistance contains trapped energy. Once you realize that the resistance in the horse are created by your ego and there is always an underlying good in every resistance, we can begin to learn from the horse. We learn to dance with the resistance and instead of blaming the horse we learn to work with our own minds to uproot the resistances we create."

- Craig Stevens
www.FoundationfortheEquestrianArts.org

Daily | S M T W TH F S ___ / ___ / 20___

Observations

....

....

Points of the Session & Diagram Space

....

....

What do you want to focus on next session?

....

....

Daily | S M T W TH F S ___ / ___ / 20___

Observations

....

....

Points of the Session & Diagram Space

....

....

What do you want to focus on next session?

....

....

Daily | S M T W TH F S ____ / ____ / 20 ____

Observations

....

....

....

Points of the Session & Diagram Space

....

....

What do you want to focus on next session?

....

....

Daily | S M T W TH F S ____ / ____ / 20____

Observations

....

....

Points of the Session & Diagram Space

....

....

What do you want to focus on next session?

....

....

"Water is fluid, soft, and yielding. But water will wear away rock, which is rigid and cannot yield. As a rule, whatever is fluid, soft, and yielding will overcome whatever is rigid and hard. This is a paradox: what is soft is strong."

- Lao Tzu

Daily | S M T W TH F S ____ /____ / 20____

Observations

....

....

Points of the Session & Diagram Space

....

....

What do you want to focus on next session?

....

....

Daily | S M T W TH F S ____ / ____ / 20____

Observations

....

....

Points of the Session & Diagram Space

....

....

What do you want to focus on next session?

....

....

Daily | S M T W TH F S ____ / ____ / 20____

Observations

....

....

Points of the Session & Diagram Space

....

....

What do you want to focus on next session?

....

....

Daily | S M T W TH F S ___ / ___ / 20___

Observations

....

....

Points of the Session & Diagram Space

....

....

What do you want to focus on next session?

....

....

"Riders with good technique can be recognized by their relaxed but focused attitude in the saddle. They have a pattern they work by, and they stick to it. They are completely coordinated with the horse and handle potential problems by actually forestalling them. They make the difficult movements look fluid and easy. These days, with the heightened sophistication in the sport, everyone can produce the movements. What impresses and wins in the end is the performance when the rider makes it all look easy!"

- Anne Gribbons,
"The Power of the Seat"

Daily | S M T W TH F S ____ / ____ / 20 ____

Observations

Points of the Session & Diagram Space

What do you want to focus on next session?

Daily | S M T W TH F S ____ / ____ / 20____

Observations

....

....

Points of the Session & Diagram Space

....

....

What do you want to focus on next session?

....

....

Daily | S M T W TH F S ___ / ___ / 20___

Observations

....

....

Points of the Session & Diagram Space

....

....

What do you want to focus on next session?

....

....

Daily | S M T W TH F S ____ / ____ / 20____

Observations

Points of the Session & Diagram Space

What do you want to focus on next session?

" Remember that top riders use their aids for three purposes:

First, they prepare the horse for action by shaping him and putting him in front of the leg. These are preparatory aids.

Second, they listen to the horse to see if he is ready to respond. This listening aid also is necessary for the rider to analyze the work based on the Training Scale.

Finally, when the rider knows the horse is ready, then the aids ask for action. The action aids are usually successful when the horse is prepared and the rider is listening."

- Beth Baumert,
"The Action Aids"

Daily | S M T W TH F S ___ / ___ / 20___

Observations

....

....

Points of the Session & Diagram Space

....

....

What do you want to focus on next session?

....

....

Daily | S M T W TH F S ____ / ____ / 20____

Observations

....

....

Points of the Session & Diagram Space

....

....

What do you want to focus on next session?

....

....

Daily | S M T W TH F S ____ / ____ / 20____

Observations

....

....

Points of the Session & Diagram Space

....

....

What do you want to focus on next session?

....

....

Daily | S M T W TH F S ____ / ____ / 20____

Observations

....

....

Points of the Session & Diagram Space

....

....

What do you want to focus on next session?

....

....

"Submission is a word that indicates something negative and, unfortunately, it is sometimes interpreted in a bad way by forcing a horse to obey.

But if one puts the partnership with a horse in the center of his equitation, the kind of submission we are talking about is a positive one gained by suppling the horse to an extent that he is moving in balance and, as a result, willingly executes what we ask him to do."

- Colonel Christian Carde,
"Walk: The Queen of Gaits"

Daily | S M T W TH F S ___ / ___ / 20___

Observations

....

....

Points of the Session & Diagram Space

....

....

What do you want to focus on next session?

....

....

Daily | S M T W TH F S ____ / ____ / 20____

Observations

....

....

Points of the Session & Diagram Space

....

....

What do you want to focus on next session?

....

....

Daily | S M T W TH F S ____ / ____ / 20____

Observations

Points of the Session & Diagram Space

What do you want to focus on next session?

Daily | S M T W TH F S ____ / ____ / 20 ____

Observations

Points of the Session & Diagram Space

What do you want to focus on next session?

"A horse will never tire of a rider who possesses both tact and sensitivity because he will never be pushed beyond his possibilities."

- Nuno Oliveira

Daily | S M T W TH F S ____ / ____ / 20____

Observations

....

....

Points of the Session & Diagram Space

....

....

What do you want to focus on next session?

....

....

Daily | S M T W TH F S ____ / ____ / 20____

Observations

....

....

Points of the Session & Diagram Space

....

....

What do you want to focus on next session?

....

....

Daily | S M T W TH F S ____ / ____ / 20____

Observations

_____

_____

Points of the Session & Diagram Space

_____

_____

What do you want to focus on next session?

_____

_____

Daily | S M T W TH F S ____ / ____ / 20____

Observations

Points of the Session & Diagram Space

What do you want to focus on next session?

"One thing that is appealing to horse owners, and also therapists, about the method of bodywork I use and teach is the interaction between the therapist and the horse, and the horse's involvement in the process. This isn't a mechanical process. It's a process where you learn how to read the horse. The horse talks to you, and let's you know where, how much, and when the tension is released."

- Jim Masterson
www.MastersonMethod.com

Daily | S M T W TH F S ____ / ____ / 20____

Observations

Points of the Session & Diagram Space

What do you want to focus on next session?

Daily | S M T W TH F S ____ / ____ / 20____

Observations

....

....

Points of the Session & Diagram Space

....

....

What do you want to focus on next session?

....

....

Daily | S M T W TH F S ___ / ___ / 20___

Observations

....

....

Points of the Session & Diagram Space

....

....

What do you want to focus on next session?

....

....

Daily | S M T W TH F S ____ / ____ / 20____

Observations

....

....

Points of the Session & Diagram Space

....

....

What do you want to focus on next session?

....

....

"Don't ride for what will make him look best, ride for what will make him feel best."

-Susan Leighton

Daily | S M T W TH F S ____ / ____ / 20____

Observations

Points of the Session & Diagram Space

What do you want to focus on next session?

Daily | S M T W TH F S ___ /___ / 20___

Observations

....

....

Points of the Session & Diagram Space

....

....

What do you want to focus on next session?

....

....

Daily | S M T W TH F S ____ / ____ / 20____

Observations

....

....

Points of the Session & Diagram Space

....

....

What do you want to focus on next session?

....

....

Daily | S M T W TH F S ____ /____ / 20____

Observations

....

....

Points of the Session & Diagram Space

....

....

What do you want to focus on next session?

....

....

"So as we became more aware of the emotions of our horses and their personalities, and opinions even, we were in fact becoming more aware of their state of mind. We understood firstly that like people, horses cannot learn or truly respond to us when they are in a state of tension.

Tension is a complicated subject. It is a state of mind which, like any state of mind, has physical effects."

Happy-Horse-Training.com

Daily | S M T W TH F S ___ / ___ / 20 ___

Observations

....

....

Points of the Session & Diagram Space

....

....

What do you want to focus on next session?

....

....

Daily | S M T W TH F S ____ / ____ / 20____

Observations

....

....

Points of the Session & Diagram Space

....

....

What do you want to focus on next session?

....

....

Daily | S M T W TH F S ____ /____ / 20____

Observations

....

....

Points of the Session & Diagram Space

....

....

What do you want to focus on next session?

....

....

Daily | S M T W TH F S ____ / ____ / 20____

Observations
_____

....

....

Points of the Session & Diagram Space
_____

....

....

What do you want to focus on next session?
_____

....

....

"Good dressage, equitation, or horseback riding requires a great deal of sensitivity. It is far easier to develop and work with mechanics and a mechanical universe than it is to make a personal commitment to the unfolding of your innate sensitivity."

- Craig Stevens
http://www.foundationfortheequestrianarts.org/

Daily | S M T W TH F S ____ / ____ / 20____

Observations

_____

....

....

Points of the Session & Diagram Space

_____

....

....

What do you want to focus on next session?

_____

....

....

Daily | S M T W TH F S ___ / ___ / 20___

Observations

....
....

Points of the Session & Diagram Space

....
....

What do you want to focus on next session?

....
....

Daily | S M T W TH F S ___ /___ / 20___

Observations

....

....

Points of the Session & Diagram Space

....

....

What do you want to focus on next session?

....

....

Daily | S M T W TH F S ___ /___ / 20___

Observations

....

....

Points of the Session & Diagram Space

....

....

What do you want to focus on next session?

....

....

"We not only need to strengthen the muscles but, in particular, the personality of the horse."

- Reiner Klimke

Daily | S M T W TH F S ____ /____ / 20____

Observations

....

....

Points of the Session & Diagram Space

....

....

What do you want to focus on next session?

....

....

Daily | S M T W TH F S ____ / ____ / 20____

Observations

Points of the Session & Diagram Space

What do you want to focus on next session?

Daily | S M T W TH F S ____ / ____ / 20 ____

Observations

....

....

Points of the Session & Diagram Space

....

....

What do you want to focus on next session?

....

....

Daily | S M T W TH F S ___ / ___ / 20___

Observations

_____

....

....

Points of the Session & Diagram Space

_____

....

....

What do you want to focus on next session?

_____

....

....

"Only ask for a couple of steps in the beginning. Build the horse's confidence that he can do the work we are asking of him. We can always build on that."

-Mark Russell

Daily | S M T W TH F S ____ / ____ / 20____

Observations

Points of the Session & Diagram Space

What do you want to focus on next session?

Daily | S M T W TH F S ____ / ____ / 20____

Observations

....

....

Points of the Session & Diagram Space

....

....

What do you want to focus on next session?

....

....

Daily | S M T W TH F S ____ /____ / 20____

Observations

Points of the Session & Diagram Space

What do you want to focus on next session?

Daily | S M T W TH F S ____ /____ / 20____

Observations

....

....

Points of the Session & Diagram Space

....

....

What do you want to focus on next session?

....

....

"The reason most people give up is because they tend to look at how far they still have to go, instead of how far they have come."

- Unknown

Daily | S M T W TH F S ____ / ____ / 20____

Observations

....

....

Points of the Session & Diagram Space

....

....

What do you want to focus on next session?

....

....

Daily | S M T W TH F S ____ / ____ / 20____

Observations
_____

....

....

Points of the Session & Diagram Space
_____

....

....

What do you want to focus on next session?
_____

....

....

Daily | S M T W TH F S ____ / ____ / 20____

Observations

....

....

Points of the Session & Diagram Space

....

....

What do you want to focus on next session?

....

....

Daily | S M T W TH F S ____ / ____ / 20____

Observations

Points of the Session & Diagram Space

What do you want to focus on next session?

"Let your horse experience a sense of success at the end of the session and ask it to do an exercise that it can do particularly well or that he likes doing. Because your horse does not forget the impression it leaves the arena with, it is likely to start off again the next day with exactly the same feelings when it enters the arena."

- Anja Beran

Daily | S M T W TH F S ____ / ____ / 20____

Observations

Points of the Session & Diagram Space

What do you want to focus on next session?

Daily | S M T W TH F S ___ / ___ / 20___

Observations

....

....

Points of the Session & Diagram Space

....

....

What do you want to focus on next session?

....

....

Daily | S M T W TH F S ____ / ____ / 20____

Observations

_____

....

....

Points of the Session & Diagram Space

_____

....

....

What do you want to focus on next session?

_____

....

....

Daily | S M T W TH F S ____ /____ / 20____

Observations

....

....

Points of the Session & Diagram Space

....

....

What do you want to focus on next session?

....

....

" There is a reason for "equitation skills", and it is not to look pretty. Equitation is about the physics of thrust and speed and balance and motion, and how the human body either gets in the way of the horse as he does his job, or gets out of his way so he can function."

- Denny Emerson

Observations

....

....

Points of the Session & Diagram Space

....

....

What do you want to focus on next session?

....

....

Observations

Daily | S M T W TH F S ____ / ____ / 20____

Observations

....

....

Points of the Session & Diagram Space

....

....

What do you want to focus on next session?

....

....

CONGRATULATIONS!

Well done! You've just completed your Equestrian Journal. It's a great feeling of accomplishment and now there is literally a book written about your horse. I hope you'll keep up the good work!

Visit www.TheEquestrianJournal.com to purchase your next journal. We offer Accelerator Journal Coaching, 3 types of journal bindings, a digital journal to use on your tablet or phone, many alternative page options, and custom designed journals. Please let me know if you have any specific requests or would enjoy a custom option for your program. I love hearing from my "journalers."

Be sure to check out our Certified Partner Program - it's a sprinkle of sponsorship, a dash of affiliate alliance, and a big scoop of added value to the services offered by educators, clinicians, bodyworkers, coaches, and trainers.
 https://www.theequestrianjournal.com/partnerships

For the Horse,

Catherine Respess

RREFERENCES

American Psycholgy Associations's Journal of Experimental
Psychology: General (JEP: General) (Vol. 130, No. 3)

Weibell, C. J. (2011). Principles of learning: 7 principles to guide personalized, student-centered learning in the technology-enhanced, blended learning environment. Retrieved July 4, 2011 from [https://principlesoflearning.wordpress.com].

Mueller, P. A., & Oppenheimer, D. M. (2014, April 23). The Pen Is Mightier Than the Keyboard . Re-

Made in the USA
Monee, IL
08 December 2020